My Anxiety-Free Life:

Discovering Inner Peace and Liberation from Anxiety and Depression

By

Amber R. Walls

Copyrights ©2023 Amber R. Walls
All Rights Reserved

Table of Contents

Introduction

A Glimpse into the Storm: The Stranglehold of Anxiety

Anxiety is like that unwelcome guest who overstays their welcome. It's not just a fleeting feeling; it's a constant presence, like a cloud that never seems to lift. I've had my fair share of encounters with this inner storm, and let me tell you, it's no walk in the park.

Picture this: you're going about your day, minding your own business, when suddenly your heart starts racing like it's in a marathon. Your chest tightens, and you're left feeling like you're on the edge of something terrifying. The funny thing is, there's often no real reason for it. Your mind just decides to send out an alarm signal for no apparent cause.

And that's just the beginning. This storm of anxiety can turn the simplest decision into a mental battlefield. You second-guess yourself, dissecting every word and action like you're under a microscope. Did I say the right thing? Did I come across as awkward? It's like you're playing a never-ending game of social chess, and you're convinced that everyone else is a grandmaster.

Sleep? Oh, good luck with that. The nighttime is when anxiety throws its wildest party. Suddenly, your brain becomes a nightclub for your worries, and you're the unwilling DJ. Your mind keeps replaying all the things that went wrong during the day and conjures up new catastrophes for you to chew on. It's as if your pillow becomes a confessional booth for your fears.

What's worse is that the storm blinds you to the world around you. The little pleasures in life, like the taste of your morning coffee or the feel of a warm breeze, fade into the background. Your mind is so preoccupied with what might happen that it forgets to savor what's happening right now. It's like watching a movie but being too caught up in analyzing the plot to actually enjoy it.

But don't let this sound all gloomy. In the midst of this chaotic weather, there's a ray of hope peeking through the clouds. It's the realization that anxiety doesn't define you; it's just a part of your story. You start discovering tools that help you wrestle back some control, like taking deep breaths, practicing mindfulness, or talking it out with a friend.

"A Glimpse into the Storm" isn't a tale of defeat; it's a story of resilience. It's about acknowledging that yeah, anxiety is a tough customer, but it's not unbeatable. It's about learning to dance in the rain, even when the storm rages on. And let's be real, life is full of storms. Embracing this journey means embracing the fact that you're stronger than you think, and that even in the midst of chaos, you can find pockets of peace.

Chapter 1: Seeds of Anxiety

Ever notice how some of the biggest things in life start out as the tiniest, most inconspicuous beginnings? Well, anxiety's got that same sneaky way of working its way into your life. I call them the "Seeds of Anxiety" – those seemingly innocent moments from way back when that somehow managed to grow into something much bigger.

You know, it's funny how those early memories stick with you. I remember being a kid, and there was this one time I had to give a presentation in front of the class. My heart raced, my palms got all sweaty – it was like my body was staging a mutiny against me. Little did I know, that was a seed being planted, one that would sprout into a whole garden of anxiety in the future.

Then there were those playground days, making friends and all that. But there were moments when I felt like I didn't quite fit in, like I was a puzzle piece that just didn't belong in the picture. Those moments, though seemingly harmless, were actually little hints that maybe I wasn't as confident as I wanted to be. Those hints turned into nagging doubts, and before I knew it, they were part of that garden too.

It's kind of crazy how these tiny incidents can take root and shape the way we see the world. That garden of anxiety grew over the years, watered by more moments of self-doubt and worry. Suddenly, everyday decisions became tough choices, and I found myself overthinking things that others seemed to breeze through.

But you know what? Realizing that these moments were the seeds helped me see things differently. It wasn't that I was destined to be anxious forever – I just had some early experiences that had a bigger impact than I thought. And just like you can prune a plant to help it grow better, I could work on pruning those negative thought patterns and beliefs.

"Seeds of Anxiety" isn't a doom-and-gloom chapter; it's more like the backstory to the main event. It's about understanding that anxiety isn't some mysterious monster that appeared out of thin air. It had its beginnings, and those beginnings can help us find our way out. It's about shining a light on those little moments from the past and realizing that they don't have to define our present or our future.

So yeah, maybe anxiety planted its seeds early on, but now I've got the gardening gloves on. I'm tending to my mental garden, pulling out the weeds of self-doubt and nurturing the flowers of confidence. Because just as those seeds had the power to grow into something bigger, I've got the power to shape what grows next.

Early Experiences and Their Lasting Impact

Remember those days when everything seemed new, and the world was this big, uncharted territory waiting to be explored? Those early experiences, no matter how insignificant they might have seemed at the time, have this uncanny ability to stick with us and shape the people we become. But you know what's interesting? They also have a way of leaving a mark on our emotional landscape – and for me, that meant dealing with the lasting impact of anxiety.

And then there were the times I felt like I didn't quite fit in. The birthday parties where I felt like the odd one out, the group activities where I was convinced I was the weakest link – these moments might have faded into the past, but their echoes reverberated through the years. They laid the groundwork for self-doubt, whispering that I wasn't good enough or that I'd always be on the fringes.

It's fascinating how these seemingly ordinary moments from childhood have a way of casting long shadows. They're like puzzle pieces that fit together to create a bigger picture of who we are. Those early experiences taught me lessons about how I should navigate the world, even if I wasn't aware of it at the time. They planted the seeds of beliefs that would grow into towering trees of thoughts and emotions.

"Early Experiences and Their Lasting Impact" isn't about pointing fingers or blaming the past. It's about understanding that we're all products of our history, shaped by the moments that made us laugh, cry, or cringe. It's about peeling back the layers to see how those experiences left their fingerprints on our hearts and minds. It's about recognizing that while we can't change the past, we can certainly change how we perceive and respond to it.

And you know what? That realization is a double-edged sword. On one hand, it can be a sobering reminder that some of our challenges have deeper roots than we might have thought. On the other hand, it's incredibly empowering because it means that we're not prisoners of our history. We have the power to rewrite our narratives, to acknowledge those early experiences, and to consciously shape our present and future in a way that aligns with who we want to be.

So, as I reflect on those early experiences and their lasting impact, I do so with a mix of nostalgia, understanding, and determination. I'm excavating the layers of my past to better understand the layers of my present. Because those moments from way back when? They're not just stories; they're the foundation upon which I'm building my story now.

Unraveling the Roots of Anxiety

Have you ever wondered why you feel the way you do? I mean, really dug deep to figure out where those emotions come from? I sure have. It's like trying to untangle a web of thoughts, fears, and worries that seem to have a life of their own. That's exactly what I set out to do when I started unraveling the roots of my anxiety – to understand where it all began and how it managed to weave itself into the fabric of my life.

Picture this: you're holding a ball of yarn, and it's a complete mess. Threads are intertwined, knotted up, and it seems impossible to find where they start or end. That's how anxiety felt for me – a jumble of emotions that I couldn't make sense of. But just like that ball of yarn, I knew there had to be a beginning, a point where all these feelings took shape.

So, armed with curiosity and a bit of trepidation, I delved into my memories. I went back to those moments that left a mark, those instances that felt like tiny pebbles tossed into a pond, creating ripples that grew bigger over time. And you know what I found? I found that the roots of my anxiety weren't in one big traumatic event but in a series of smaller moments that, when connected, painted a bigger picture.

Unraveling the roots of anxiety wasn't about blame or dwelling on the past; it was about understanding. It was about acknowledging that our emotions have a backstory, that they don't just appear out of thin air. Those roots run deep, stretching back to our early experiences, our upbringing, and the messages we absorbed along the way.

It's not always an easy journey, though. Some memories bring a smile, while others bring a twinge of discomfort. But in those uncomfortable moments, there's a glimmer of insight. It's like shining a light into the darkness, revealing the patterns and connections that we might have missed before. It's realizing that our present struggles often have their origins in the past.

"Unraveling the Roots of Anxiety" isn't about dwelling on the negative; it's about gaining perspective. It's about peeling back the layers to understand why we react the way we do and how we can rewrite our emotional script. It's about taking that tangled ball of yarn and starting to untangle it, one thread at a time.

As I journey through these memories, I'm learning that the roots of my anxiety aren't something to be ashamed of or hidden away. They're a part of my story, the backstory that adds depth and complexity to who I am.

And by understanding those roots, I'm not just unraveling the past; I'm paving the way for a more mindful and empowered future.

Chapter 2: The Breaking Point

Struggling in Silence: Living with Unmanaged Anxiety

Imagine being stuck in a room with a thousand thoughts, all competing for your attention at once. That's what living with unmanaged anxiety feels like. It's like being trapped in a whirlwind of worries, unable to find a way out. And the worst part? It's a struggle that often happens behind closed doors, in the shadows of silence.

For the longest time, that's where I found myself – grappling with a storm of emotions while wearing a mask of composure. On the surface, everything might have seemed fine, but beneath that façade, I was constantly battling the torrents of anxiety that threatened to consume me. It was like walking a tightrope, always teetering on the edge of unraveling.

Every day became a mission to keep the anxiety hidden, to make sure no one saw the chaos within. It was exhausting – mentally, emotionally, and even physically. I'd put on a brave face, engage in conversations, go through the motions of life, all while carrying the weight of fear and worry. And as the days turned into weeks, and the weeks into months, the silence grew heavier.

The thing about unmanaged anxiety is that it's not just about the racing heartbeats or the sleepless nights. It's about the constant doubts that swirl around in your mind. It's about that nagging feeling that no matter what you do, it's not enough. It's the fear of judgment, the fear of being labeled as "weak" or "overreacting."

Living with unmanaged anxiety is like walking on eggshells, always cautious, always on guard. It's turning down invitations to social events because you're not sure you'll fit in. It's canceling plans at the last minute because your mind has conjured up a hundred worst-case scenarios. It's being your own harshest critic, replaying conversations and analyzing every word, looking for signs that you've somehow messed up.

But here's the thing: silence doesn't have to be the norm. Struggling in silence isn't a life sentence. It's a phase, a chapter that can be rewritten. It's about realizing that you don't have to bear this burden alone, that there are people who care and who want to help.

"Struggling in Silence: Living with Unmanaged Anxiety" isn't just a story of hardship; it's a story of recognition. It's about acknowledging that you deserve support, that your emotions are valid, and that you're not alone in this journey. It's about stepping out of the shadows and seeking the help you need – whether it's through therapy, talking to a friend, or simply giving yourself permission to be vulnerable.

As I reflect on those days of struggling in silence, I'm reminded that there's strength in opening up. Sharing your experiences, your fears, and your hopes is a step towards healing. It's about breaking down the walls of isolation and letting in the light of understanding. Because the truth is, you're not defined by your struggle; you're defined by how you choose to overcome it.

When the Walls Came Crashing Down: The Turning Point

Life has a way of humbling us when we least expect it. For me, that humbling moment arrived like a wrecking ball, shattering the walls of denial and self-preservation that I had painstakingly built. It was the turning point – the instant when the facade cracked, and I had no choice but to confront the reality of my unmanaged anxiety.

I had become quite the expert at masking my inner turmoil. To the outside world, I was the composed one, the dependable friend, the person who had it all together. Inside, however, I was drowning in a sea of worries, each wave threatening to pull me under. I thought I could handle it all on my own, that I could keep those walls standing strong forever.

But life has a funny way of showing you your limits. It was a seemingly ordinary day, much like any other, when everything changed. The stressors that had been piling up suddenly became too heavy to bear. It was as if my mind had reached its breaking point, unable to carry the weight of unspoken fears and unchecked emotions any longer.

That day, the walls that I had constructed so carefully came crashing down, leaving me exposed and vulnerable. I found myself in a state of emotional chaos, unable to suppress the torrent of feelings that had been building up for so long. The tears that I had been holding back for ages flowed freely, washing away the façade and the illusion of control.

It was a painful moment, but it was also a liberating one. As I sat amidst the rubble of my emotional fortress, I realized that I had been living a lie – to others and, perhaps more importantly, to myself. The turning point wasn't just about acknowledging the depth of my anxiety; it was about accepting that I couldn't continue down this path of isolation and self-deception.

In that vulnerable moment, I discovered a newfound strength. I realized that asking for help wasn't a sign of weakness, but an act of courage. I reached out to a close friend and shared my struggles, my fears, and my overwhelming emotions. And you know what? The response wasn't judgment or pity; it was empathy, understanding, and a reminder that I wasn't alone in this journey.

"When the Walls Came Crashing Down: The Turning Point" isn't just a chapter of vulnerability; it's a testament to the power of surrender. It's about understanding that sometimes, it takes the breakdown of old structures to build something stronger and more authentic. It's about realizing that hitting rock bottom can be the foundation for a new beginning.

As I reflect on that pivotal moment, I'm reminded that even amidst the ruins of our most carefully constructed defenses, there's an opportunity for growth. It's in those shattered pieces that we find the fragments of our true selves, ready to be pieced together with honesty, support, and a newfound commitment to facing our challenges head-on.

Chapter 3: Seeking Help

Reaching Out: The Courage to Ask for Support

They say that asking for help is a sign of strength, but in a world that often celebrates independence and self-sufficiency, it can feel like quite the opposite. For me, reaching out for support was a journey of rediscovering what real strength truly means – a journey that required courage, vulnerability, and a willingness to let others into the innermost corners of my struggles.

Admitting that I needed help was no small feat. It meant acknowledging that I couldn't handle everything on my own, that my well-constructed facade of strength was just that — a facade. But as I stood at the crossroads, faced with the choice of continuing down the path of isolation or opening up to those who cared about me, I realized that true strength lay in the latter.

Reaching out for support wasn't a sign of weakness; it was a testament to my determination to take control of my narrative. It was the decision to shatter the illusion of self-sufficiency and to embrace the truth that none of us are meant to navigate life's challenges alone. It was acknowledging that seeking help wasn't a failure; it was a step toward growth and healing.

The process wasn't without its anxieties. Would I be judged? Would my struggles be dismissed as insignificant? These questions echoed in my mind as I approached a close friend, baring my soul and sharing the unfiltered reality of my emotions. It was a vulnerable moment, a leap into the unknown, but the response I received was nothing short of a lifeline.

Instead of judgment, I found empathy. Instead of dismissal, I found understanding. The act of sharing my burden with another human being lifted a weight I hadn't realized I had been carrying. It was as if a veil of isolation had been lifted, revealing a network of connections and a web of support that I hadn't fully appreciated.

"Reaching Out: The Courage to Ask for Support" is more than a chapter in my story; it's a lesson in human connection. It's about understanding that strength isn't measured by how much we can handle on our own, but by our willingness to lean on others when the load becomes too heavy. It's about recognizing that we all have moments when we need a helping hand, and that seeking that hand is a declaration of self-care and self-respect.

As I reflect on the journey of reaching out, I'm reminded that the act of vulnerability has a remarkable ability to foster intimacy and understanding. It's about breaking down the walls that keep us separate and realizing that by sharing our struggles, we invite others to share theirs. It's about creating a safe space where authenticity is celebrated, and where the courage to ask for support becomes a beacon of hope for others facing similar challenges.

Navigating the World of Therapy and Treatment

Entering the world of therapy and treatment can feel like embarking on a journey to uncharted territory. It's a realm that's often shrouded in misconceptions and uncertainties, yet it holds the promise of a path towards understanding, healing, and growth. As I stepped into this world, I discovered that it was a space of immense opportunity, one where I could finally start unpacking the complexities of my anxiety.

Therapy – just saying the word can trigger a mix of emotions. For some, it's a beacon of hope, a chance to address long-standing issues and gain insights into their inner workings. For others, it might be met with skepticism or even fear, fueled by societal stigmas or personal reservations. But for me, therapy became a lifeline, a space where I could lay bare my thoughts and emotions without fear of judgment.

The journey began with finding the right therapist – someone who felt like the right fit, someone with whom I could share my struggles openly and honestly. It wasn't an easy process, and there were moments of doubt and uncertainty. But when I finally connected with a therapist who felt like a supportive partner on my journey, it was like finding a compass in the wilderness.

Therapy, I realized, was more than just talking about my problems. It was a collaborative effort, a process of self-discovery guided by a trained professional. It was a safe space where I could explore the roots of my anxiety, unpack the thought patterns that had held me captive, and develop coping strategies to navigate life's challenges. It wasn't about "fixing" me; it was about empowering me to navigate the complexities of my emotions.

As I navigated the world of therapy, I also learned the value of patience. Progress wasn't always linear, and there were moments of frustration when it felt like I was taking steps backward. But my therapist was there to remind me that healing is a journey, not a destination. The insights I gained and the tools I acquired began to seep into my daily life, guiding me through moments of uncertainty and helping me manage anxiety's grip.

"Navigating the World of Therapy and Treatment" is more than a chapter in my story; it's a testament to the power of seeking help and embracing the process of growth. It's about breaking down the barriers that might have kept me from seeking treatment and recognizing that therapy isn't a sign of weakness but a step towards empowerment.

As I reflect on this part of my journey, I'm reminded that therapy is a partnership built on trust, honesty, and a shared commitment to healing. It's about stepping into the unknown with an open heart and a willingness to face the shadows within. It's about allowing ourselves to be vulnerable and recognizing that in our vulnerability lies our strength.

Chapter 4: Tools for Transformation

Unveiling Coping Strategies: From Breathing Exercises to Mindfulness

When anxiety tightens its grip, it can feel like you're trapped in a whirlwind of thoughts and emotions, desperately searching for a lifeline. That's where coping strategies come in – those tools and techniques that offer a way to navigate the stormy seas of anxiety. From simple breathing exercises to the profound practice of mindfulness, these strategies became my allies on the journey towards reclaiming a sense of control and tranquility.

Breathing exercises – they might sound simple, but their impact can be profound. The act of consciously focusing on each breath, of inhaling deeply and exhaling slowly, has this magical ability to anchor you in the present moment. It's like your breath becomes a lifeline, pulling you out of the tumultuous waters of anxiety and into the calm shores of the here and now.

Mindfulness, on the other hand, took me on a journey within. It's a practice of being fully present, of observing your thoughts and emotions without judgment. At first, it felt a bit strange – like trying to tame a wild horse that had been running amok in my mind. But with time and practice, I discovered that mindfulness allowed me to create a space between myself and my thoughts. It was like stepping back and realizing that I wasn't defined by my anxious thoughts; I was simply experiencing them.

Then there's the power of reframing – a way to shift your perspective and reinterpret the situations that trigger anxiety. It's about asking yourself, "What's the worst that could happen?" and then challenging those worst-case scenarios with a dose of reality. Suddenly, the monsters under the bed start to lose their power, and you realize that many of your fears are based on assumptions rather than facts.

And let's not forget the importance of self-care. It's like nurturing your own garden – tending to your emotional well-being with the same care you'd give to a cherished plant. Whether it's taking a walk, indulging in a favorite hobby, or simply giving yourself permission to rest, self-care is a reminder that you deserve moments of peace and rejuvenation.

"Unveiling Coping Strategies: From Breathing Exercises to Mindfulness" isn't just about listing techniques; it's about understanding that you have an arsenal of tools at your disposal. It's about recognizing that you're not helpless in the face of anxiety – you have the power to respond in ways that promote calm and resilience.

As I reflect on my journey with these coping strategies, I'm reminded that managing anxiety isn't about erasing it entirely; it's about developing the skills to navigate its waves. It's about embracing the ebb and flow of emotions while anchoring yourself in practices that bring you back to a place of inner strength. It's about realizing that you have the power to soothe the storms within and uncover a sense of peace that was always there, waiting to be discovered.

The Power of Journaling: Unpacking Emotions and Finding Clarity

Have you ever felt like your mind was a cluttered attic, filled with thoughts and emotions that needed sorting? That's exactly how I felt before discovering the transformative power of journaling. It's like having a secret confidant – a blank page that listens without judgment, allowing you to pour out your thoughts and emotions in their raw, unfiltered form.

Journaling became my sanctuary, a safe space where I could unravel the tangle of thoughts that often left me feeling overwhelmed. It was a simple act – pen to paper – but its impact was profound. As I began to write, the floodgates of my mind opened, and the words flowed like a stream of consciousness. It was liberating to give voice to the thoughts that had been silently wreaking havoc within me.

What amazed me was how journaling provided clarity. It was as if the act of translating my thoughts into words gave them shape and form. It allowed me to step back and see my emotions from a different perspective, almost like an outsider looking in. Suddenly, the chaotic jumble of thoughts began to organize itself into a narrative that I could make sense of.

And you know what else? Journaling gave me a space to challenge my thoughts. It was a platform to question my anxieties, to ask myself if my fears were based on reality or if they were simply the product of an overactive imagination. It was a way to play detective with my emotions, sifting through the evidence and debunking the myths that anxiety often weaves.

But perhaps the most powerful aspect of journaling was its role in fostering self-compassion. Writing allowed me to treat myself with the kindness and understanding that I so easily extended to others. It was a reminder that my struggles weren't unique or shameful – they were part of the human experience. Through the pages of my journal, I found a way to be gentle with myself, to acknowledge my challenges without judgment.

"The Power of Journaling: Unpacking Emotions and Finding Clarity" isn't just about scribbling down thoughts; it's about creating a dialogue with yourself. It's about giving a voice to the inner chatter that often goes unnoticed. It's about recognizing that your thoughts and emotions deserve space and validation, even if they're messy or uncomfortable.

As I reflect on the role of journaling in my journey, I'm reminded that sometimes, the simplest acts can have the most profound impact. Journaling became my compass, guiding me through the labyrinth of my emotions. It became a tool of self-discovery, a companion on the path to understanding and healing. And in the process, it taught me that sometimes, the act of putting pen to paper can lead to revelations that were hiding in plain sight all along.

Chapter 5: Embracing Change

Stepping Stones to Progress: Overcoming Challenges and Setbacks

Life has a way of throwing curveballs when you least expect it. Just when you think you're making progress, challenges and setbacks come knocking, testing your resilience and determination. But what if I told you that these obstacles aren't roadblocks but stepping stones on the path to growth? That's what I've come to understand as I've navigated the ups and downs of my journey to manage anxiety.

Challenges can feel like heavy weights on your shoulders, threatening to push you down. They can trigger old patterns of thinking, resurfacing doubts and fears that you thought you had left behind. It's easy to feel disheartened, to wonder if all the progress you've made was for naught. But here's the thing – challenges are opportunities in disguise.

Each challenge is a chance to put your coping strategies to the test, to apply the tools you've learned along the way. It's an invitation to show yourself just how far you've come, to prove to yourself that you're more resilient than you might have believed. While challenges can be uncomfortable and even painful, they also offer a chance for growth and self-discovery.

Setbacks, on the other hand, can be discouraging. It's like taking a few steps backward just when you thought you were moving forward. But setbacks aren't the end of the road; they're detours that can lead you to unexpected insights. They remind you that progress isn't always linear, that healing is a journey of ups and downs.

As I faced challenges and setbacks, I learned the importance of self-compassion. It's easy to be hard on yourself, to berate yourself for not handling things perfectly. But setbacks are a reminder that you're human – you're allowed to stumble, and you're allowed to take a moment to regroup. Self-compassion means treating yourself with the same kindness you'd offer to a friend in a similar situation.

"Stepping Stones to Progress: Overcoming Challenges and Setbacks" isn't just about adversity; it's about resilience. It's about understanding that progress isn't a smooth ride but a journey that's punctuated by hurdles. It's about recognizing that setbacks are opportunities to refine your strategies and to cultivate a sense of inner strength that can weather even the toughest storms.

As I reflect on the challenges and setbacks I've faced, I'm reminded that each one has contributed to my growth. They've taught me patience, self-compassion, and the power of adaptability. They've shown me that progress isn't about avoiding obstacles but about using them as stepping stones towards a stronger, more resilient self. And so, I continue to move forward, knowing that with each challenge conquered and each setback overcome, I'm writing my own story of triumph over adversity.

Embracing a Lifestyle of Self-Care and Wellness

In a world that often glorifies hustle and burnout, the concept of self-care and wellness can feel like a much-needed breath of fresh air. For me, it's been a journey of shifting my priorities, of recognizing that taking care of my mental, emotional, and physical well-being isn't just a luxury – it's a necessity. Embracing a lifestyle of self-care and wellness has been a transformative experience that has helped me navigate the complexities of anxiety and daily life.

Self-care isn't just about spa days and bubble baths (although those can be wonderful). It's about intentionally carving out time to nurture your soul, to listen to your needs, and to replenish your energy. It's about acknowledging that you're not a machine; you're a human being with emotions, limits, and the right to prioritize your well-being.

For me, self-care became a ritual of self-compassion. It's about checking in with myself regularly and asking, "What do I need right now?" Sometimes, it's a quiet moment with a cup of tea and a good book. Other times, it's a walk in nature or a creative outlet that allows me to express my emotions. Self-care isn't a one-size-fits-all concept; it's about finding what resonates with you and making it a non-negotiable part of your routine.

Wellness, on the other hand, encompasses a holistic approach to health – not just the absence of illness, but a state of thriving. It's about nourishing your body with balanced nutrition, staying active in ways that bring you joy, and prioritizing sleep and rest. It's also about nurturing your mind, whether through mindfulness practices, therapy, or engaging in activities that stimulate your intellectual curiosity.

Embracing a lifestyle of self-care and wellness means recognizing that you deserve to thrive, not just survive. It's about shedding the guilt that sometimes accompanies taking time for yourself and understanding that investing in your well-being isn't selfish; it's an act of self-love. It's about realizing that by taking care of yourself, you're better equipped to show up for others and contribute positively to the world around you.

"Embracing a Lifestyle of Self-Care and Wellness" isn't just about routines; it's about a mindset shift. It's about choosing to prioritize your health and happiness, even in a world that might push you to the sidelines. It's about understanding that self-care isn't an indulgence; it's an essential part of living a balanced and fulfilling life.

As I reflect on my journey towards self-care and wellness, I'm reminded that it's a continuous process. It's not about perfection; it's about progress. It's about honoring yourself, your needs, and your boundaries, and creating a life that aligns with your values. And in that journey, I've found that the more I embrace self-care and wellness, the more I find the strength to navigate the challenges that come my way with a sense of grace and resilience.

Chapter 6: Building Resilience

From Victim to Victor: Cultivating Inner Strength

Life has a way of throwing curveballs, and sometimes, it feels like we're at the mercy of circumstances beyond our control. I used to feel like a victim of my own anxieties, powerless to their grip. But then, something shifted – a transformation that took me from being a victim to becoming a victor, cultivating a wellspring of inner strength that I didn't know I had.

Cultivating inner strength isn't about being invulnerable or never experiencing fear or doubt again. It's about developing a resilience that allows you to face challenges head-on, to bounce back from setbacks, and to rise above adversity. It's a journey of rewiring your mindset, shifting from a place of powerlessness to one of empowerment.

For me, this transformation began with a shift in perspective. I realized that while I couldn't always control the situations I found myself in, I could control how I responded to them. Instead of seeing myself as a victim of anxiety, I started to view myself as someone who could actively engage with it, someone who could learn and grow from the experience.

This shift wasn't immediate or effortless. It required consistent effort and a willingness to step out of my comfort zone. It meant facing my fears gradually, challenging the beliefs that had held me back, and gradually building a foundation of confidence. It was about acknowledging that anxiety was a part of me, but it didn't define me.

The process of cultivating inner strength also involved building a toolbox of coping strategies. It was like assembling an armor of techniques that I could turn to when anxiety struck – from mindfulness practices that anchored me in the present to reframing techniques that challenged my anxious thoughts. Each strategy became a tool that reinforced my sense of agency and control.

But perhaps the most significant aspect of this journey was learning to be my own champion. It's about embracing self-compassion, recognizing that I'm not perfect and that setbacks are a natural part of growth. It's about celebrating my victories, no matter how small, and acknowledging the progress I've made. It's about finding my voice and using it to advocate for myself and my well-being.

"From Victim to Victor: Cultivating Inner Strength" is more than a chapter in my story; it's a mantra for life. It's about understanding that while we can't control everything, we can control how we respond. It's about realizing that we have the power to transform our mindset and rewrite our narrative. It's about recognizing that inner strength isn't something you're born with; it's something you nurture, cultivate, and harness in the face of life's challenges.

As I reflect on my journey from victim to victor, I'm reminded that cultivating inner strength is a lifelong process. It's about continually building resilience, deepening self-awareness, and embracing the journey of personal growth. It's about discovering that within us lies a wellspring of strength that can carry us through even the stormiest of seas, reminding us that we are not just survivors – we are victors in our own story.

Harnessing Adversity as a Catalyst for Growth

Adversity – it's a word that often carries a negative connotation. We tend to associate it with challenges, struggles, and discomfort. But what if I told you that adversity has the potential to be a catalyst for growth, a force that can push us beyond our limits and propel us towards transformation? That's the lesson I've learned as I've navigated the twists and turns of my journey.

Adversity isn't just a roadblock; it's a crossroads. It's a moment when we're faced with a choice – to succumb to the weight of the challenge or to rise above it. It's in those moments of adversity that we're presented with an opportunity to dig deep, to tap into reserves of strength we might not have known existed.

I've come to see adversity as a teacher – a tough, demanding teacher who pushes us to learn and grow. It's in facing challenges that we discover our true potential, the depths of our resilience, and the scope of our capabilities. Adversity forces us to step outside our comfort zones, to stretch and expand, and to develop skills and perspectives we might never have cultivated otherwise.

But here's the secret: growth often requires discomfort. It's like the discomfort of a seed breaking open to sprout into a tree. Adversity can be that breaking point, the moment when we shed old limitations and reach towards the sunlight of progress. It's about embracing discomfort as a sign of growth, as a signal that we're on the verge of becoming something more.

I've also found that adversity brings clarity. It's like a magnifying glass that highlights what truly matters. In the face of challenges, we're forced to evaluate our priorities, to discern what's essential and what's expendable. Adversity can strip away the trivial and the superficial, leaving us with a profound understanding of our values and goals.

"Harnessing Adversity as a Catalyst for Growth" is a chapter that doesn't just tell a story of struggle; it tells a story of triumph. It's about understanding that adversity isn't a roadblock that stops us; it's a path that propels us forward. It's about embracing the bumps along the way and seeing them as stepping stones towards a stronger, more resilient version of ourselves.

As I reflect on the role of adversity in my journey, I'm reminded that challenges don't define us – how we respond to them does. Adversity can be the spark that ignites a fire within us, motivating us to strive for greatness. It can be the wind beneath our wings, carrying us to heights we never thought possible. And in that process, we find that adversity isn't just an obstacle; it's a vehicle for growth, a catalyst that transforms us into versions of ourselves that we can be truly proud of.

Chapter 7: Reconnecting with Joy

Rediscovering Passions and Hobbies

In the hustle and bustle of life, it's easy to lose sight of the things that once brought us joy – those passions and hobbies that used to light up our souls. As I navigated the challenges of managing anxiety, I found that rediscovering these sparks of passion became an unexpected source of healing and rejuvenation.

Passions and hobbies are like forgotten treasures buried beneath the demands of daily life. They're the activities that make your heart race with excitement, that allow you to lose yourself in the flow of the moment. For me, rekindling these flames meant reconnecting with parts of myself that anxiety had overshadowed.

It started with a simple question: "What used to make me happy?" The answer wasn't always immediate, but as I delved into the memories of my past, I unearthed a trove of interests that had taken a backseat. It was like finding old friends – the kind that you reconnect with effortlessly, as if no time had passed.

Rediscovering passions and hobbies was more than just a distraction; it was a form of self-care. It was about carving out time for activities that fed my soul and brought a sense of accomplishment. Whether it was painting, playing a musical instrument, or immersing myself in books, these pursuits became a refuge from the chaos of anxiety.

Engaging in these activities was like hitting the reset button on my mind. It was a chance to escape the cycle of anxious thoughts and immerse myself in the present moment. The absorption was so complete that, for a time, my worries took a backseat. It was a reminder that there was a world beyond anxiety, a world waiting to be explored and enjoyed.

But perhaps the most profound aspect of rediscovering passions and hobbies was the sense of empowerment it brought. As I honed my skills and immersed myself in creative pursuits, I felt a surge of confidence. It was a reminder that anxiety didn't define me; I was a multi-faceted individual with talents and interests that extended beyond my worries.

"Rediscovering Passions and Hobbies" is more than a chapter; it's a celebration of self-discovery. It's about acknowledging that even in the midst of challenges, there's space for joy and creativity. It's about recognizing that investing in activities that bring you happiness isn't a luxury – it's an essential part of nurturing your well-being.

As I reflect on the role of passions and hobbies in my journey, I'm reminded that they're not just distractions; they're sources of vitality and inspiration. They're reminders that life is a tapestry woven with threads of diverse experiences, and that taking time to engage in activities that make your heart sing is a form of self-love. Through rediscovering these passions, I found a way to infuse my life with color, purpose, and a renewed sense of vitality.

Fostering Meaningful Relationships: The Role of Connection

In a world that's increasingly interconnected yet often feels isolating, the role of meaningful relationships has never been more crucial. As I embarked on my journey to manage anxiety, I discovered that the power of connection – with others and with myself – played a profound role in shaping my healing process.

Meaningful relationships aren't just about having a wide circle of friends or a bustling social calendar. They're about cultivating deep, authentic connections with people who truly see and understand you. These relationships become pillars of support, providing a safety net when the winds of anxiety threaten to knock you off balance.

I found that vulnerability was the key to forging these connections. It's about opening up, sharing your fears and struggles, and allowing others to do the same. Vulnerability can be scary – it means exposing your innermost thoughts and emotions – but it's also incredibly liberating. It's through vulnerability that you create bonds that are built on empathy, understanding, and a shared sense of humanity.

Connection, however, isn't just about others; it's also about reconnecting with yourself. Anxiety often leads to a disconnect between mind and body, leaving you feeling adrift. Rebuilding that connection involves cultivating self-awareness – listening to your thoughts, acknowledging your emotions, and treating yourself with the same kindness you would offer a friend.

Meaningful relationships are also a reminder that you're not alone in your struggles. It's easy to feel isolated when anxiety takes hold, but connecting with others who've faced similar challenges can be incredibly comforting. Sharing experiences, offering and receiving support, and realizing that others have triumphed over anxiety can be a beacon of hope.

But fostering meaningful relationships requires effort. It's about being present in conversations, truly listening to others, and showing up for the people in your life. It's about setting boundaries that protect your own well-being and respecting the boundaries of others. It's about quality over quantity, nurturing a few deep connections rather than spreading yourself thin.

"Fostering Meaningful Relationships: The Role of Connection" isn't just about interactions; it's about creating a sense of belonging. It's about recognizing that we're wired for connection, that human beings thrive when we're seen, heard, and understood. It's about acknowledging that meaningful relationships aren't just a nice-to-have; they're a fundamental aspect of our emotional well-being.

As I reflect on the impact of connection in my journey, I'm reminded that the support of loved ones and the bonds of shared experiences have been lifelines. They've shown me that healing isn't a solitary endeavor; it's a collaborative journey. They've taught me that the act of reaching out and building bridges of understanding is an affirmation of our shared humanity. Through fostering these meaningful relationships, I've discovered that even in the midst of anxiety's storm, there are anchors of connection that can help us weather the turbulence and find solace in the embrace of those who truly care.

Chapter 8: The Journey to Acceptance

Redefining Normalcy: Embracing Imperfections

In a world that often glorifies perfection and success, the idea of redefining normalcy can be both liberating and transformative. As I navigated the labyrinth of managing anxiety, I discovered that embracing imperfections – in myself and in life – was a key to unlocking a deeper sense of acceptance and self-love.

Society often sets unrealistic standards for what constitutes "normal." It's a pressure cooker of expectations that can leave us feeling inadequate, as if we're constantly falling short. But what if our imperfections were not something to be hidden or ashamed of, but aspects that make us uniquely human? This shift in perspective can be a balm for the soul, a reminder that we're all on a journey, and none of us have it all figured out.

Embracing imperfections is about recognizing that life is beautifully messy. It's like admiring a patchwork quilt – each piece, though different, contributes to the overall tapestry of our experiences. It's in the imperfections that we find character, depth, and stories that shape who we are. It's about celebrating the quirks and idiosyncrasies that make us individuals, rather than striving for a cookie-cutter version of normal.

But this redefinition isn't just about accepting the external imperfections; it's about embracing the internal ones too. Anxiety can often make us feel flawed, as if our worries and fears are somehow abnormal. But the truth is, anxiety is a common thread that runs through the fabric of humanity. Acknowledging it, talking about it, and seeking help when needed is a sign of strength, not weakness.

Redefining normalcy also means rewriting the narrative of success. It's about realizing that success isn't just about achievements and accolades; it's about growth, resilience, and the ability to navigate life's challenges with grace. It's about shifting from a mindset of comparison to one of self-compassion, understanding that everyone's journey is unique and valid.

"Redefining Normalcy: Embracing Imperfections" isn't just a chapter in my story; it's a mantra for living. It's about understanding that our imperfections don't define us; they enrich us. It's about recognizing that the pursuit of perfection is a futile endeavor that robs us of the opportunity to fully engage with life as it is.

As I reflect on the role of imperfections in my journey, I'm reminded that they're not just flaws; they're facets of authenticity. They're invitations to let go of pretense and embrace vulnerability. They're reminders that it's okay to stumble, to make mistakes, and to be a work in progress. Through redefining normalcy, I've learned that imperfections aren't something to be hidden; they're the threads that weave the beautiful tapestry of a life fully lived.

Embracing Uncertainty: Navigating Life's Twists and Turns

Life is a journey filled with twists and turns, surprises and uncertainties. In a world where we often seek control and predictability, learning to embrace uncertainty can be a daunting yet incredibly freeing endeavor. As I faced the challenges of managing anxiety, I discovered that the ability to navigate life's uncertainties became a valuable skill that fostered resilience and personal growth.

Uncertainty can be uncomfortable – it's like stepping into the unknown without a roadmap. It can trigger anxiety, making us feel like we're standing on shaky ground. But what if we reframed uncertainty as an adventure? An opportunity to explore, learn, and adapt? This shift in perspective invites us to step forward with curiosity rather than fear.

Embracing uncertainty is about acknowledging that we can't control every outcome. It's like releasing the tight grip we have on life's steering wheel and allowing the current to guide us. It's a surrender to the idea that change is a constant, and rather than resisting it, we can learn to flow with it. This acceptance can lead to a sense of liberation, as we let go of the need for rigid plans and instead open ourselves to the possibilities that lie ahead.

Uncertainty also teaches us resilience. Just as a tree bends with the wind rather than breaking, learning to adapt to life's unpredictability builds our inner strength. It's about developing the flexibility to adjust our sails when the winds of change blow us off course. This adaptability becomes a wellspring of strength in times of challenge, reminding us that we've weathered storms before and emerged stronger on the other side.

Moreover, embracing uncertainty invites us to be present in the moment. When we're fixated on a predetermined outcome, we miss out on the richness of the journey itself. Uncertainty encourages us to be mindful, to savor the experiences as they unfold, and to find beauty in the unexpected detours. It's a reminder that life is happening now, and our ability to fully engage with it brings a sense of fulfillment and wonder.

"Embracing Uncertainty: Navigating Life's Twists and Turns" is more than a chapter; it's a philosophy for living. It's about recognizing that uncertainty is not a barrier to overcome but a facet of existence to be embraced. It's about learning to dance in the rain instead of waiting for the storm to pass.

As I reflect on my journey of embracing uncertainty, I'm reminded that life's uncertainties are opportunities for growth. They're the soil in which resilience takes root, and the canvas upon which our stories are painted. By leaning into uncertainty, we discover that the journey itself is the destination, and that every twist and turn is a stepping stone on the path of self-discovery.

Chapter 9: Empowerment and Advocacy

Advocating for Mental Health: Sharing Your Story and Breaking Stigma

In a world that often shrouds mental health in silence and stigma, the act of advocating for our well-being can be a revolutionary act. As I confronted the challenges of managing anxiety, I came to understand the transformative power of sharing my story and breaking the chains of stigma that had held me – and countless others – captive.

Advocating for mental health isn't just about talking about disorders and diagnoses; it's about sharing the human experience. It's about acknowledging that emotions are a part of being alive and that struggling with them doesn't make us weak. By opening up, we invite others to do the same, creating a space where authenticity and vulnerability are celebrated.

Breaking the stigma surrounding mental health begins with our stories. It's about peeling back the layers and revealing the challenges we've faced, the battles we've fought, and the triumphs we've celebrated. When we share our stories, we show that mental health is a common thread that connects us all. We shatter the illusion that we're alone in our struggles and pave the way for a community of support.

Advocacy is a ripple effect. When one person speaks out, it emboldens others to do the same. It's a domino effect that gradually erodes the walls of shame and secrecy that stigma builds. By advocating for mental health, we become torchbearers for change, lighting a path for those who come after us to walk a little more freely, a little more openly.

But advocacy isn't just about speaking; it's about listening. It's about creating a safe space for others to share their stories, knowing that they won't be met with judgment or dismissal. It's about lending an empathetic ear and offering a shoulder to lean on. It's about reminding each other that our experiences are valid and that seeking help is a sign of strength, not weakness.

"Advocating for Mental Health: Sharing Your Story and Breaking Stigma" isn't just a chapter; it's a call to action. It's about understanding that our voices have the power to create change, to chip away at the walls of stigma that have confined mental health to the shadows. It's about recognizing that every story shared, every conversation started, is a step towards a more compassionate and inclusive world.

As I reflect on my journey of advocacy, I'm reminded that by sharing our stories, we become beacons of hope for others who are navigating similar challenges. Our stories have the potential to save lives, to offer solace, and to create a ripple effect of understanding and acceptance. By advocating for mental health, we become agents of change, dismantling the barriers that keep us from fully embracing our humanity.

Paying It Forward: Supporting Others on Their Journey

As I walked the winding path of managing anxiety, I came to understand that the journey wasn't just about my own healing — it was also about supporting others who were treading similar paths. "Paying it forward" took on a new meaning as I realized the profound impact of offering a helping hand to those who were navigating their own challenges.

Supporting others on their journey isn't about having all the answers or being a perfect guide. It's about showing up with empathy, compassion, and a willingness to listen. It's about creating a space where people can share their thoughts and feelings without fear of judgment. It's about saying, "I see you, I hear you, and you're not alone."

Just as others had extended their support to me, I felt a responsibility to offer the same to those who were struggling. Whether through a kind word, a listening ear, or simply being a presence in someone's life, supporting others became a way of turning my own experiences into something meaningful and purposeful.

Paying it forward is a ripple effect of healing. When we offer our support, we become a beacon of hope for others. We remind them that even in the darkest moments, there's a glimmer of light. Our words and actions can be lifelines, helping someone find their way back to the surface when they're drowning in their thoughts.

But paying it forward isn't just about offering support in times of crisis; it's also about celebrating victories and milestones. It's about cheering each other on as we take steps towards our goals. It's about reminding each other of our resilience and our capacity to overcome. It's about being a source of encouragement and strength.

"Paying It Forward: Supporting Others on Their Journey" isn't just a chapter; it's a commitment to the human experience. It's about recognizing that none of us have all the answers, but we all have the ability to make a positive impact. It's about understanding that by lifting others up, we're also elevating ourselves and creating a web of interconnected support.

As I reflect on the role of supporting others in my journey, I'm reminded that healing isn't just an individual endeavor; it's a collective one. Our stories, our experiences, and our challenges are threads that weave us together. By paying it forward, we contribute to a tapestry of empathy, understanding, and shared humanity. Through supporting others, I found a way to give meaning to my own struggles and to be a part of something greater than myself.

Chapter 10: The New Chapter

Reflecting on the Transformation: How Far You've Come

As I stand at the threshold of my journey, it's hard not to marvel at the distance I've traveled. The path I've walked to manage anxiety has been marked by challenges, triumphs, and moments of profound self-discovery. As I reflect on this transformation, I'm struck by how far I've come – not just in terms of managing anxiety, but in the evolution of my entire being.

Looking back, it's clear that every step I've taken has been a building block, each experience a brick in the foundation of my growth. The struggles I faced weren't roadblocks; they were opportunities for me to develop resilience, to learn coping strategies, and to deepen my understanding of myself. Each victory, no matter how small, added a layer to my armor of inner strength.

Reflecting on this transformation isn't just about recognizing the progress made in managing anxiety; it's about acknowledging the growth that has rippled through every aspect of my life. The skills I've cultivated in managing my mental health have spilled over into my relationships, my work, and my overall sense of well-being. It's like a ripple effect of positive change that has touched every corner of my existence.

But transformation is not just about accomplishments; it's also about a shift in mindset. The way I view challenges has changed. Instead of seeing them as insurmountable obstacles, I now see them as opportunities for growth. I've learned to embrace uncertainty, to find beauty in imperfection, and to approach life with a sense of curiosity and openness. This shift has brought a newfound sense of freedom and authenticity to my journey.

Reflecting on the transformation is also a reminder that the journey is ongoing. Healing isn't a destination; it's a continuous process of growth and self-discovery. The tools and strategies I've learned along the way are not just for navigating anxiety; they're life skills that will continue to serve me in the years to come. Every day is an opportunity to build upon the progress I've made and to continue shaping the narrative of my own story.

"Reflecting on the Transformation: How Far You've Come" is more than a chapter; it's a celebration of personal evolution. It's about recognizing that growth is not a linear path but a tapestry of experiences, emotions, and moments of self-realization. It's about understanding that the journey is as significant as the destination and that every step forward is a testament to my resilience and determination.

As I reflect on how far I've come, I'm filled with a sense of gratitude – for the challenges that pushed me to grow, for the victories that validated my efforts, and for the journey itself. The transformation is ongoing, and I step forward with a heart full of hope, a mind filled with curiosity, and a spirit that's ready to embrace whatever comes next.

Embracing the Future: Living a Life Free from the Grip of Anxiety

As I stand on the cusp of the future, a profound sense of liberation washes over me. The journey to manage anxiety has been a road of self-discovery, growth, and transformation. Now, as I gaze ahead, I'm filled with a quiet confidence that the future is mine to shape, a canvas waiting to be painted with colors of hope, resilience, and possibility.

Embracing the future is not about erasing the past; it's about carrying the lessons learned, the strength gained, and the wisdom acquired into the uncharted territory ahead. It's about approaching life with a renewed sense of purpose, armed with the tools to navigate challenges and savor victories. It's about stepping forward with the knowledge that I am more than the sum of my anxieties.

The future beckons with open arms, a landscape of opportunities waiting to be explored. It's an invitation to dream, to set goals, and to chase aspirations with a newfound fervor. The resilience I've developed in managing anxiety is not just a shield to protect me; it's a beacon that guides me as I chart my course and pursue my passions.

Embracing the future is also about letting go of the weight of worry and stepping into a world of possibility. It's about understanding that anxiety does not define me; it's a part of me, but it doesn't hold the reins anymore. It's about rewriting the narrative of my life – a story where empowerment, growth, and joy take center stage.

The future is a canvas awaiting my touch, and I am the artist of my destiny. It's a journey where I can continue to build meaningful relationships, celebrate victories, and learn from challenges. It's a voyage where I can pay forward the support and understanding I've received, creating a ripple effect of empathy and compassion.

"Embracing the Future: Living a Life Free from the Grip of Anxiety" is not just a conclusion; it's a new beginning. It's a testament to the power of resilience, the beauty of transformation, and the boundless potential of the human spirit. It's about stepping forward with courage, embracing uncertainty, and believing in the strength I've cultivated within myself.

As I stand at the threshold of the future, I am reminded that the journey is ongoing. The pages of my story are waiting to be written, and I am both the author and the protagonist. With gratitude for the past, hope for the present, and excitement for the future, I step forward, ready to embrace life's tapestry of experiences, to create my own narrative, and to live a life free from the grip of anxiety.

Conclusion: Writing the Story of Resilience and Hope

As I close the final chapter of this book, I'm reminded of the incredible journey we've embarked upon together. It's been a journey of self-discovery, growth, and transformation – a journey that has taken us through the depths of anxiety and into the realm of empowerment, resilience, and hope.

Throughout these pages, we've explored the intricate layers of managing anxiety, unraveling its roots, and discovering the tools to navigate its challenges. We've delved into the power of embracing imperfections, fostering meaningful connections, and rewriting the narratives that hold us back. We've seen how vulnerability can be a source of strength, and how supporting others is a path to healing ourselves.

The chapters of this book aren't just words on paper; they're stories woven together to create a tapestry of shared experiences and shared humanity. From the early seeds of anxiety to the triumph of cultivating inner strength, from the storms of uncertainty to the embrace of a brighter future – each chapter has illuminated a facet of the journey we all traverse.

Through the highs and lows, the victories and setbacks, one common thread has emerged: the power of the human spirit. It's the spirit that drives us to face our fears, to seek support, and to rewrite our stories. It's the spirit that transforms adversity into catalysts for growth, that redefines normalcy, and that empowers us to pay it forward.

As we close this book, remember that your journey is ongoing. The story of resilience and hope doesn't end here; it's a narrative that you'll continue to shape with every step you take. Your experiences, challenges, and triumphs are part of a collective tapestry that connects us all.

May you carry the wisdom you've gained, the strength you've cultivated, and the compassion you've embraced into your future endeavors. May you find solace in the moments of uncertainty and joy in the milestones you achieve. And may you always remember that you are not defined by your anxieties, but by your ability to rise above them.

Thank you for allowing me to be a part of your journey. As you close this chapter and open the next, I wish you resilience, courage, and a life filled with the vibrant colors of hope and possibility. You are the author of your story, and your story is one of transformation, strength, and the unwavering light of hope.

- ## Resources for Managing Anxiety

1. Professional Support:

Therapy: Cognitive Behavioral Therapy (CBT), Dialectical Behavior Therapy (DBT), and mindfulness-based therapies can be effective in managing anxiety.
Counseling: Speaking with a licensed counselor or therapist provides a safe space to explore your thoughts and emotions.

2. Self-Care Practices:

Mindfulness and Meditation: Techniques like deep breathing, guided meditation, and mindfulness exercises can help ground you in the present moment.
Exercise: Regular physical activity releases endorphins and helps reduce stress and anxiety.

Sleep Hygiene: Prioritizing quality sleep enhances your ability to manage stress.

3. Support Groups and Communities:

Local Support Groups: Connecting with others who understand your struggles can provide a sense of belonging and validation.
Online Communities: Virtual platforms offer a space to share experiences, find encouragement, and access resources.
4. Journaling and Expressive Arts:

Journaling: Writing down your thoughts and emotions can provide clarity and promote self-reflection.
Art and Creativity: Engaging in creative activities like drawing, painting, or crafting can be therapeutic.

5. Apps and Digital Resources:

Mindfulness Apps: Apps like Headspace, Calm, and Insight Timer offer guided meditation and relaxation exercises.
Cognitive Behavioral Apps: Tools like Woebot and MoodKit provide CBT-based techniques to manage anxious thoughts.

6. Reading and Learning:

Books: There are numerous books on anxiety management, self-help, and personal growth that can provide insights and practical strategies.
Online Resources: Websites, blogs, and articles offer a wealth of information on coping with anxiety.

7. Relaxation Techniques:

Breathing Exercises: Practicing deep breathing techniques can help reduce stress and induce a sense of calm.

Progressive Muscle Relaxation: This technique involves tensing and then relaxing different muscle groups to release tension.

8. Lifestyle Factors:

Healthy Diet: A balanced diet rich in nutrients can support mental well-being.
Limiting Stimulants: Reducing caffeine and sugar intake can help stabilize mood.

Remember, building a toolkit takes time and experimentation. What works for one person might not work for another, so be patient and open to trying different approaches. Combining various strategies and seeking professional guidance can lead to a more holistic and effective approach to managing anxiety. Your journey is unique, and these resources are here to support you every step of the way.

<u>Acknowledgments</u>

As I pen down the final words of this book, I am reminded that no journey is ever traveled alone. The path to managing anxiety, and the creation of this book, has been illuminated by the support, encouragement, and love of many remarkable individuals. With heartfelt gratitude, I extend my appreciation to those who have played an integral role in bringing these pages to life:

To my Family:
Your unwavering support and understanding have been my anchor throughout this journey. Your patience, love, and belief in me have been a source of strength that words cannot fully express.

To my Friends:
Thank you for the laughter, the late-night conversations, and the shared moments of

vulnerability. Your presence has been a constant reminder that I am never alone.

To my Mentors:
Your guidance, wisdom, and encouragement have been invaluable. Your insights have shaped not only my understanding of anxiety but also my perspective on life's challenges.

To my Therapist:
Your compassion, empathy, and expertise have been instrumental in helping me navigate the complexities of anxiety. Your guidance has provided me with tools that extend far beyond the pages of this book.

To the Writing Community:
Your feedback, insights, and camaraderie have enriched the writing process in ways I could not have anticipated. Your collective passion for storytelling has been a source of inspiration.

To the Readers:
Your willingness to engage with this book is a gift beyond measure. It is my hope that these pages provide you with insights, comfort, and the knowledge that you are not alone on your journey.

To the Team:
The dedication, hard work, and creative vision of the team that brought this book to life is deeply appreciated. Your commitment to the project has transformed words into a tangible reality.

To Those Who Shared Their Stories:
Your courage in sharing your experiences with anxiety has been a reminder that vulnerability is a catalyst for connection and change. Your stories have contributed to the tapestry of this book.

To My Inner Self:
You have shown me strength I never knew I possessed. You have weathered storms and

celebrated victories. Through every moment, you have persevered with determination and hope.

With gratitude in my heart, I extend my deepest appreciation to each and every individual who has been a part of this journey. May your kindness and support continue to ripple through the lives of others, just as it has touched mine.

With warmth and gratitude,

Amber R. Walls

<u>About the Author</u>

Amber R. Walls is a compassionate storyteller and advocate for mental health awareness. With a background in psychology and a passion for writing, Amber has embarked on a journey to illuminate the intricate nuances of the human experience, particularly the challenges and triumphs of managing anxiety.

Amber's dedication to understanding the human psyche led her to explore the complexities of anxiety in both personal and academic realms. Through extensive research, introspection, and a commitment to breaking down the barriers of stigma, she has woven together a narrative that resonates with authenticity and compassion.

With a keen understanding of the transformative power of words, Amber's writing transcends the page, inviting readers to connect with their own emotions and experiences. Her ability to convey vulnerability and strength alike has earned her a place in the hearts of those navigating their own journeys through anxiety and self-discovery.

Amber's work is not limited to the realm of writing; she actively contributes to the mental health community through her advocacy efforts. Her dedication to fostering meaningful connections and supporting others on their paths to healing reflects her commitment to building a more empathetic and inclusive world.

As an author, advocate, and beacon of hope, Amber R. Walls has taken her personal journey of managing anxiety and transformed it into a narrative that empowers, enlightens, and uplifts. Through her words, she extends a hand to those who may be struggling, reminding them that they are not alone and that there is strength to be found in vulnerability.

With her heart on the page and her gaze fixed on a brighter future, Amber R. Walls continues to inspire, educate, and create spaces where the human experience is honored, celebrated, and understood.

www.ingramcontent.com/pod-product-compliance
Lightning Source LLC
Chambersburg PA
CBHW070915260726

48661CB00004B/1739